Born Again:
What does it really mean?

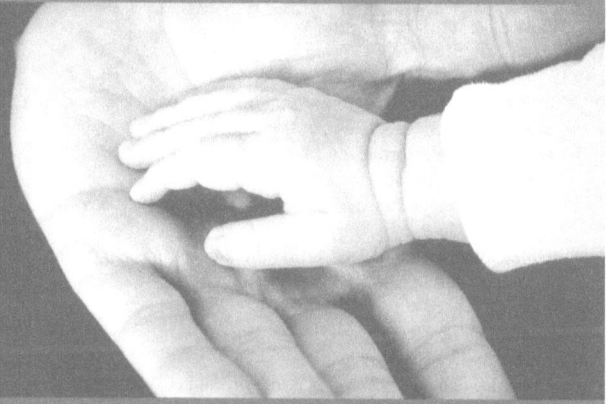

Dr Shaun Marler

Born Again – What Does It Really Mean?
Copyright © 2004
Dr Shaun Marler

Published by:
World Harvest Ministries, PO Box 90,
Bald Hills, Qld, 4036, Australia
whm.org.au

This book or parts thereof may not be reproduced in any form, stored in a retrieval system, or transmitted in any form, by any means - electronic, mechanical, photocopy, recording or otherwise - without prior written permission of the author or publisher, except as provided by Australian copyright law.

Unless otherwise indicated, all scripture quotations are taken from the King James Version of the Bible.

Written by Dr Shaun Marler
Edited by Ps Peter Howlett
Cover Design by Jay Binks & Sarah Freeman
Photo by Canva

First Published October 2020

ISBN: 978-0-6485897-6-1

This Book is Dedicated to the Seeker.

God Loves You And Has A Wonderful Plan for Your Life.
(Jeremiah 29:11,12)

I pray that as you read this book, you discover the One who loves you, and that in that discovery, you enter into a personal relationship with Him. If we never meet on this earth, I pray that some day we meet on the streets of gold, in the eternal Kingdom.

Love in Jesus,
Shaun

Thank You

To everyone who has helped me prepare this little book, I extend my gratitude and special thanks. Together we can, love more, reach more, do more and win more for Jesus.

Introduction

As the cover says, "Born again, what does it really mean?" This small book's purpose is to introduce you to the God, the Creator of all things, and His Son the Lord Jesus Christ.

My prayer for you is, that as you read these words contained in these pages, you find the One Who created you. He loves you so much, that He came and paid the price for you to live forever with Him in eternal bliss and paradise.

Jesus said, *"Seek, and you will find. Knock, and the door will be opened. Ask and you will receive."*

You are at the beginning of an exciting journey that will lead to eternal life.

You can also discover and learn more by downloading our App or visiting our web page at whm.org.au.

Join the Family

God has a wonderful plan for your life. He wants you to be a part of His eternal family. Just like you were born into your earthly family, you must be born into God's family. God loves you so much that He sent His Son, the Lord Jesus Christ, to die for you - even if you have no earthy family of your own. He did this so that you can be adopted into His family.

Let's have a look at what the Bible says about being born again:

"There was a man of the Pharisees, named Nicodemus, a ruler of the Jews; The same came to Jesus by night, and said unto Him, 'Rabbi, we know that You are a teacher come from God: for

no man can do these miracles that You do, except God be with Him.'

Jesus answered and said unto him, 'Truly, Truly, I say unto you, except a man be born again, he cannot see the kingdom of God'. Nicodemus said unto Him, 'How can a man be born when he is old? Can he enter the second time into his mother's womb, and be born?'

Jesus answered, 'Truly, Truly, I say unto you, except a man be born of water *(natural childbirth)* and of the Spirit *(spiritual birth)*, he cannot enter into the kingdom of God. That which is born of the flesh is flesh; and that which is born of the Spirit is Spirit. Marvel not that I said unto you, you must be born again. The wind blows where it wills, and you hear the sound thereof, but cannot tell where it comes from and where it goes: so is every one that is born of the Spirit."
John 3:1-8

From the previous verses, we can see that Jesus told one of the most religious men of His day, Nicodemus, that he must be born again in order for him to see the Kingdom of God. Nicodemus had come to Jesus one night to enquire about this new doctrine (teaching). Nicodemus was a Pharisee, and a ruler of the Jews. He believed in God, he prayed, fasted, tithed, and attended worship services. He tried to keep high moral standards, yet even with all of these things going for him, Jesus still told him that in order to enter the Kingdom of God, he must be born again.

You see, it is **"not by works of righteousness that we have done that saves us, but we are saved according to His mercy by the washing of regeneration and renewing of the Holy Spirit."** *Titus 3:5*

In the Book of *Romans 3:23,* it tells us every person has sinned and come short of the glory of God.

"For the wages of sin is death, but the gift of God is eternal life through Jesus Christ our Lord". *Romans 6:23*

Here we can see that the penalty of our sin is death (separation from God), but the free gift of God is eternal life through Jesus Christ our Lord.

In *Isaiah 64:6,* it tells us that **"all our righteousness is as filthy rags"** in the sight of our God.

"Therefore, by the deeds of the law, there shall no flesh be justified in His sight: for by the law is the knowledge of sin. But now the righteousness of God without

the law is manifested, being witnessed by the law and the prophets; even the righteousness of God which is by faith of Jesus Christ unto all and upon all them that believe: for there is no difference."
Romans 3:20-22

So let us just summarise the above to see what it means to be born again. We have been born as babies and grew up to the age that we are now. During the course of our lives, all of us without exception have done something wrong. When you are first born, you are born into sin, because sin is passed down through the generations - parents to children. The Bible calls this generational sin 'iniquity'. We have all made mistakes. Because of our sin (mistakes), we were separated from God, spiritually dead and doomed to an eternity without God.

BORN AGAIN - WHAT DOES IT MEAN?

"But God loved the world so much that He gave His only begotten Son, that whoever believes in Him should not perish but have everlasting life" *John 3:16*

Because of mankind's sin, God sent His Son, Jesus, into the world - not to condemn the world, but that the world, (i.e. the people of the world) might be saved through Him. Jesus Christ came, and He lived a sinless life. He went to the cross to pay the price for the transgressions (mistakes) of all people.

In the Book of *Isaiah 53:6,* it tells us that God laid on Jesus the iniquity of us all. In verses 4 and 5 of the 53rd chapter of Isaiah, we can see that **"Jesus bore our griefs, carried our sorrows, yet we did esteem Him stricken, smitten of**

God and afflicted, but He was wounded for our transgressions, He was bruised for our iniquities (sins and guilt), the punishment for our peace was upon Him, and with His stripes, we are healed".

People had sinned—sin results in death and separation from God, and ultimately eternity in hell.

"He answered and said unto them, 'He that sows the good seed is the Son of Man; the field is the world; the good seed are the children of the kingdom; but the tares are the children of the wicked one; The enemy that sowed them is the devil; the harvest is the end of the world; and the reapers are the angels. As therefore the tares are gathered and burned in the fire; so shall it be in the end of this world. The Son of man shall send forth His angels, and they shall gather out of

His kingdom all things that offend, and them which do iniquity; and shall cast them into a furnace of fire: there shall be wailing and gnashing of teeth. Then shall the righteous shine forth as the sun in the kingdom of their Father. Who has ears to hear, let him hear."
Matthew 13:37-43

Born of Water and of the Spirit

Jesus Christ came to pay the price to bridge the gap; to buy us and bring us back to God, to give us eternal life, and to make us once again God's children. You see, Jesus told Nicodemus, "You must be born again". We are born once, in our mother's womb -natural childbirth, born of water, but Jesus said we must be born again of the Holy Spirit in order to enter the Kingdom of

God. We have to make the decision - first realise that we have sinned and our sins have separated us from God and His blessings. We must then choose to repent, to turn around from going our own way, to receive Jesus as our Lord and Saviour, and to follow God through obeying His word and His will for our lives.

1 Peter 1:23 says: **"Being born again, not of corruptible seed, but of incorruptible, by the Word of God, which lives and abides for ever."**

The Word (that is the Bible) is the seed that comes into our heart and causes our faith to grow. Not only must we have God's Word in order to be born again, but also we must have God's Spirit. It is **"not by works of righteousness which we** have done, but according to His mercy He saved us, through the washing of regeneration and renewing of the Holy Spirit." *Titus 3:5*

Jesus said in *John 6:63*, "The Word that I speak unto you is spirit and it is life."

How to Be Born Again

"For by grace are you saved through faith; and that not of yourselves: it is the gift of God: Not of works, lest any man should boast." *Ephesians 2:8-9*

We could never be saved except by the pure grace (unmerited favour) of God. Man is certainly undeserving according to his own merits. It is God's power, working through His Word and Spirit that brings about new birth. Yet without the attitude of repentance and faith, God's power will not work in man's heart. Man must be obedient to God's will before he can receive God's blessings.

God's Word is God's Will

Romans 10:8-10 says; **"But what says it? The Word is near you, even in your mouth, and in your heart: that is, the Word of faith, which we preach; That if you shall confess with your mouth the Lord Jesus, and shall believe in your heart that God has raised Him from the dead, you shall be saved. For with the heart man believes unto righteousness: and with the mouth confession is made unto salvation."**

We must Believe and Confess; our faith in God's Word expressed with our heart (believe) and with our mouth (confess).

If we truly believe in our heart that God raised Jesus from the dead, there is no reason we should not be willing to confess Him as Lord. The moment someone believes in their heart upon Jesus and confesses Him as their Lord and Saviour, they are born again!

"But as many as received Him, to them gave He power to become the sons of God, even to them that believe on His name." *John 1:12*

A New Creation

"Therefore if any man be in Christ, he is a new creation: old things are passed away, behold all things have become new" *2 Corinthians 5:17*

The new birth makes us a brand new creation. We are created after the image of Jesus Christ. In our hearts, we are made to be like Christ. In order to live like Christ, we must **"put on the new man, which is renewed in knowledge after the image of him that created him:"** *Colossians 3:10*

A New Way of Living

Renewing the mind with God's Word, and submitting our bodies to the authority of that Word, will do this. To renew your mind means to replace your thoughts with God's thoughts, to think and respond as He would. God's response to us is His Word.

When we respond as the Word says, we are submitting ourselves to His Word, and in turn, submitting our bodies to Him.

"And be not conformed to this world: but be you transformed by the renewing of your mind, that you may prove what is that good, and acceptable, and perfect, will of God." *Romans 12:2*

"And be renewed in the spirit of your mind; And that you put on the new man, which after God is created in righteousness and true holiness." *Ephesians 4:23-24*

Into God's Kingdom

"Giving thanks unto the Father, who has made us fit to be partakers of the inheritance of the saints in light: WHO HAS DELIVERED US FROM THE POWER OF DARKNESS AND HAS TRANSLATED US INTO THE KINGDOM OF HIS DEAR SON: in Whom we have redemption through

His blood, even the forgiveness of sins." *Colossians 1:12-14*

When we are born again, we are taken out of Satan's kingdom of darkness, and we are placed into the Kingdom of Jesus, the Kingdom of light. It is not something we just hope or wish for. It is a fact. The child of God does not have to be lorded over by Satan ever again. Jesus makes you free from the authority of Satan.

"If the Son therefore shall make you free, you shall be free indeed" *John 8:36*

"By his death, Jesus opened a new and life-giving way through the curtain into the Most Holy Place." *Hebrews 10:20 NLT*

The Law of the Spirit of Life in Christ Jesus

This new kingdom is a spiritual kingdom; but just because salvation is basically a spiritual rebirth, does not mean that it has no effect on our bodies, minds, or everyday living. It can and should have a great impact on every part of our lives.

In every society, there are certain laws that govern the actions of the inhabitants of that area. It is the same in spiritual life. There are laws for those in this world's kingdom, and there are laws for those in God's Kingdom. The new birth gives us a new law:

"FOR THE LAW OF THE SPIRIT OF LIFE IN CHRIST JESUS has made

me free from the law of sin and death" *Romans 8:2*

The law of life includes love, joy, peace, happiness, prosperity, abundance, health, contentment, and blessings. These provisions are made for the Christian in the New Covenant. It is law; spiritual law. We must enforce it in our lives. God will back us. His Word is true and unchanging.

Forgiveness - Remission of Sins

The day we make Jesus our Lord and Saviour, we are forgiven of all our sins. In fact, we were legally forgiven when Jesus gave His life as a ransom for us. We do not, however, experience that forgiveness until we receive it by faith.

Although a person may have committed many sins, the chief sin of the unsaved is **NOT BELIEVING ON CHRIST** *(John 16:9)*. When a person gets that straightened out, the root of the problem is solved.

The blood of Christ cleanses the heart the moment a person believes and confesses Him as Saviour. All past sins are thus remitted or taken away by the powerful cleansing work of His blood.

"But if we walk in the light, as he is in the light, we have fellowship one with another, and the blood of Jesus Christ his Son cleanses us from all sin." *1 John 1:7*

"... We have redemption through His blood, the forgiveness of sins, according to the riches of His grace" *Ephesians 1:7*

There is Only One Way

Jesus is the only way by which anyone can be saved. Anyone who wants to see heaven can only do so by coming to Jesus and being born again.

"Neither is there salvation in any other: for there is none other name under heaven given among men, whereby we must be saved." *Acts 4:12*

Yet look at you now! Everything is new! Although you were once distant and far away from God, now you have been brought delightfully close to him through the sacred blood of Jesus—you have actually been united to Christ! *Ephesians 2:13 TPT*

"Jesus said unto him, I am the way, the truth, and the life: no man comes unto the Father, but by me." *John 14:6*

Here is a simple prayer that you can pray in order to be born again:

Dear Heavenly Father,

I believe that Jesus Christ is the Son of God, who has come to earth as a man. I thank you that you sent your Son, Jesus, to pay for my sins, by dying on the cross and shedding His blood for me. Jesus, I believe you rose from the dead and now I repent of my sins and ask for your forgiveness. Jesus, come into my heart by Your Spirit and be my personal Lord and Saviour. I believe with my heart and confess with my mouth that Jesus Christ is now my Lord. Father, baptize me with Your Holy Spirit and change me into the kind of person you want me to be. I am now a child of the Almighty God. Thank you for saving me.

In Jesus name, Amen.

If you prayed this simple prayer, you can know, according to God's Word that you are saved. You must believe in the promises of His Word, not your feelings, emotions or anything else. It is God's Word that guarantees your salvation.

Assurance of Salvation

"And this is the record, that God has given to us eternal life, and this life is in His Son. HE THAT HAS THE SON HAS LIFE, and he that has not the Son of God has not life. These things have I written unto you that believe on the name of the Son of God; THAT YOU MAY KNOW that you have eternal life, and that you may BELIEVE ON THE NAME of the Son of God" *1 John 5: 11-13*

"Jesus said, 'I am the Resurrection and the Life. He that believes in Me, though he were dead, yet shall he live. And whosoever lives and believes in Me shall never die'." *John 11:25, 26*

God's Promises to You

God will finish what he has started in you when you are born again. He will never leave you nor forsake you and will be there for you in every circumstance, to see you through into victory.

"Being confident of this very thing, that he which has begun a good work in you will perform it until the day of Jesus Christ." *Philippians 1:6*

"for he has said, I will never leave thee, or forsake thee." *Hebrews 13:5*

"Now unto him that is able to keep you from falling, and to present you faultless before the presence of his glory with exceeding joy." *Jude 1:24*

"Looking to Jesus the Author and Finisher of our faith, who for the joy that was set before Him endured the cross, despising the shame, and sat down at the right hand of the throne of God." *Hebrews 12:2*

"And I give them eternal life, and they shall never lose it or perish throughout the ages. *[To all eternity they shall never by any means be destroyed.]* **And no one is able to snatch them out of My hand."** *John 10:28*

"Therefore He is able also to save to the uttermost (completely, perfectly, finally, and for all time and eternity) those who

come to God through Him, since He is always living to make petition to God and intercede with Him and intervene for them." *Hebrews 7:25*

I have found that one of the most powerful ways to learn God's Word is to memorize Bible verses. The Bible says to keep God's Word before your eyes and in the middle of your heart. We could say in the middle of your focus of attention. (see Joshua 1:8)

1. Write out and memorize *Romans 3:23*.

....
....
....

2. Write out and memorize *Romans 6:23*.

....
....
....

3. Write out and memorize *1 John 1:9*.

....
....
....

4. In a few short words, answer the following question:

How do you know that you are saved?

....
....
....

Date......................

This day, I .... committed my life to the Lord Jesus Christ, and according to God's Holy and infallible Word, I was born again, and I became a part of the family of God. From this day, I will pray and read the Bible and seek God's ways for my life. For I know and am assured that God has wonderful things in store for me.

Signed...

Personal Notes...............................

BORN AGAIN - WHAT DOES IT MEAN?

"Whosover shall call on the name of the Lord shall be saved" *Acts 2.21*

Now you are saved (born again), start praying to the Father, in Jesus' Name

Jesus Gave Us an Example Prayer

He said "When you pray, pray after this manner, say 'Our father (God is now your Father) **who lives in heaven, may Your Holy name be honoured. May Your kingdom come, let Your will be done on earth as it is in heaven. Give us today the food we need, forgive us the wrongs we have done, as we forgive the wrongs that others have done to us. Do not bring us to hard testings, but keep us safe from evil and the evil one. For Yours is the kingdom, the power and the glory for ever. In Jesus' name. Amen'."** *Matt 6:9-15 Paraphrased from GNB.*

START GROWING

Now find a good church that boldly preaches God's Word and obeys it. Become part of a church family who will love and care for you, as you love and care for them. We need to be connected to each other. It increases our strength in God. It is God's plan for us. Make it a habit to pray to God each day and to read the Bible. Become a doer of the Word - a person who is blessed in their doing. Keep in contact with us. Write, email, or visit our website **www.whm.org.au**. We have many teaching aids to help equip you in life, so you can know and understand all about this new life that God has for you.

Author's Final Note...

If you have prayed the simple prayer in this book, and believed in the Lord Jesus Christ, you are now a Christian, and part of the wonderful family of God. God loves you and cares for you. He desires the very best for you and today you can begin to receive God's best in your own life. God's Word says it's yours, through what Jesus achieved for you at Calvary, so get ready to receive! We would love to know of your decision to follow the Lord Jesus Christ, contact us so we can rejoice with you and pray for you.

God bless,

Dr. Shaun Marler

Footnotes

Scripture from the KJV bible has been modernized by the author for reading and understanding purposes. E.g. *'He that hath the Son hath life'*, has been changed to, *'He that has the Son has life'*.

There are many modern translations of the bible. Visit your local Christian bookstore or online store, where you will be able to purchase a copy that you will find easy to read and understand, to start your new life in Christ.

"For the preaching of the cross is to them that perish foolishness; but unto us who are saved it is the power of God." *1 Cor 1:18.* The author encourages the reader to look up the scripture verses in this book, read and study them in context with the chapter.

CONNECT WITH US

For other information and a complete list of products, or to find out how you can support the ministry of Dr. Shaun Marler and World Harvest Ministries, contact:

P.O. Box 90 Bald Hills 4036
Phone: +61 7 3261 4555
(9am -5pm EST Aust)
Web: www.whm.org.au
Email: general@whm.org.au

A great place to start learning more about your new life in Christ and growing in your knowledge of Him, is by obtaining a copy of Dr. Shaun's book, *"Life Changing Principles For Victorious Living"* (highly recommended reading). Details are on the next page.

Also by Dr. Shaun Marler

Life Changing Principles For Victorious Living: *Keys to Unlock Your New Life in Christ* Forewords by noted authors, Jerry Savelle, Col Stringer and Jim Kilbler.

Praise Power: *The Key to Happiness* Foreword by Dr Reg Klimionok.

Both books are available on Amazon, as well as other online bookstores around the world!

BORN AGAIN - WHAT DOES IT MEAN?

ABOUT THE AUTHOR

Dr Shaun Marler is the Senior Pastor and co-founder with his wife Kerrie of World Harvest Ministries, an international organisation based in Queensland, Australia, World Harvest Ministries is committed to carrying out the Great Commission of Jesus our Lord. Taking the healing word to the nations and feeding the hungry, visiting prisoners, clothing the naked, visiting the widows and orphans in their affliction, and preaching the Good News to the poor.

World Harvest Ministries currently has programs in Australia, Africa and India, where the poor and destitute are given free medical treatment, orphan homes where children are fed, accommodated and educated, a ministry to widows who have been abandoned by society and a program to feed people with leprosy.

A portion of the proceeds of the sale of this book goes towards this valuable work, which is making a huge difference in the lives of others!

BORN AGAIN - WHAT DOES IT MEAN?

www.ingramcontent.com/pod-product-compliance
Lightning Source LLC
Chambersburg PA
CBHW020913020526
44107CB00075B/1807